Ink

Ink

poems by
Lane Mochow

Poetic Justice Books
Port St. Lucie, Florida

©2020 Lane Mochow

book design and layout: SpiNDec, Port Saint Lucie, FL
cover image: *Hair Rail (Gone)*, ©2019 Kris Haggblom

All rights reserved.

No part of this book may be used or reproduced in any manner whatsoever without written permission except in the case of brief quotations embodied in critical articles and reviews. Members of educational institutions and organizations wishing to photocopy any of the work for classroom use, or authors, artists and publishers who would like to obtain permission for any material in the work, should contact the publisher.

Printed in the United States of America.
Published by Poetic Justice Books
Port Saint Lucie, Florida
www.poeticjusticebooks.com

ISBN: 978-1-950433-48-3

FIRST EDITION
10 9 8 7 6 5 4 3 2 1

contents

The Tree	3
Ah, To Paint	5
Missing You	6
Hospital Jesus	7
I Came So Close	8
Panic	9
Tornado	10
Residency	11
Sweet Pea	12
Purple Sadness	13
We Are On A Riot	14
Tired	15
My First Marriage	16
Gasoline	17
Hospital	19
Frantic	20
Pepper Spray	22
Azaleas	24
A Garden	25
Saltamus	26
Kudzu	27
The Bonnaroo Tattoo	28
Things I Have Never Understood	29
Stars	31

Ink

The Tree

Come closer, closer
Lean your head into this page.
Notice ink, paper.
Feel Earth within it, the pulp
Of a tree long lost.
Feel its roots seep down within soil.

Think of the tire swing
This tree could have held.
Can you feel the wind
Propelling forward and backward,
Tug and push?
Can you see the little boy
Sweaty from swinging
Reading about girls falling
From the sky, plunging
Into spoke of an iron fence?
Life and death sweeping
in and out so quickly.
Tug and push.

Maybe you wonder
If a poem is worth
Saw blade to a tree.
Maybe you wonder
At sacrifice of a life.
Maybe you know
That sacrifice is necessary for art,
Maybe not. Who knows?
What I do know is the way

Lane Mochow

My heart swells at the words
Of a lover, weeps at the words
Of a death in the family.
I know that words have power,
And all I can do is pray that these words
Will move you in a new and surprising way.

Ah, to Paint

I like to play with the primary colors:
slowly blend them into greens and browns.
They twirl and smudge across the palate,
unprepared for the page.

I go to the local coffee shop, and
I see in shapes and colors.
I want to five-minute sketch
the whole shop, angle by angle; pencil
every nose, cup, frown, streak of
sunlight that trails lazily into the room.

I wear no beret, but if I owned one
I might, just to feel as if I mattered.
I've only been doing this since November
of last year: 10 months now.
I suppose I ought to be good enough
for the canvas, but every time
I try I end up throwing
it away too soon after.

Maybe one day I'll be able to comprehend
the way white lightens every shade,
diluting the old with the mastery of
millions of years of experience, since
the very spark that began the universe.

Lane Mochow

Missing You

When I miss you it feels like nothing.
Like I'm just this mellow palindrome,
no matter which way you spell it out
it still hits a B- Minor- 7th.
When I miss you I feel like when I was baptized,
submerged in a warm body of airless nothing - don't breathe in.
I want to claw my fingernails into the clay earth
and whistle through my bronchioles just to get it out.
To feel something. To expose some deeper feeling of loss,
and mourn with it, stroke its flaxen hair.

For in those moments we delve in,
deeper than the nothing, get past that,
we find our raw nakedness, ultimate vulnerability.
We can sob freely, because what we feel
is no longer a secret, but a celebration.
A reveling in emotion,
a revealing of the deeper self.

Hospital Jesus

When I met the Jesus
He took my hand, kissed it.

He told me He was Jesus
Born with black skin.

He didn't tell me to follow Him,
To fall before his feet, to kneel low.

He told me my name
Meant "Heaven on Earth".

He didn't tell me I was hell bound,
Destined for smoky flames and torment.

He told me my nose hairs
Helped me smell the supernatural.

He told me I would be His
Sixteenth consort and bear His first child.

He told me He never truly died,
Just fell into an unconscious dreamscape.

I Came So Close

I came so close
To death
    Tying the noose-knot
    White knuckled, but resolute
    Praying to God for it to end.

To love
    Tying the marital knot
    Swelling in my chest,
    Praying to God for it to last.

To think that the same hands that held her
    Held the rope,
    Dropped the rope,
    Called my father.
        Really puts things into perspective.

Panic

You can't see it from the outside.
I look fine, swaying to the music
limping through the truck's stereo system
down that Tennessee highway.
Then out of nowhere, I am bent over,
hands pressed firmly against my ears.

You can't see the fire alarm wailing,
can't sneak a glance at the way the radio dial
has my heart pounding through my fingertips.
You can't look into the panicked thoughts.
"We took that curve pretty fast."
"What if we crash?"
"We are definitely going to crash."
"There's no way you could save him."
*"He'd be gone, and it'd be your fault for not doing
    anything about it."*

"I.. I understand." I sputter.
I understand you
can't always console me.
I understand you
have your own stressors.
I understand you
are stretched thin with work and school.
I understand it's
not your job to take care of me.
You have to understand
I'm learning how to take care of myself.

Tornado

There was a time
when the sun tongued your curls just so,
and the clouds draped themselves around your hips.
When you were my entire world.

There was a time
when you were the only person I spoke to all day.
When you were my entire world.

I'm in a place
where I need to swing my hips until I start a tornado,
the warm air hitting the cold just so.
Where I need to become my entire world.

Residency

Hallucinations are not something
you can just plow through; it's singing.
It's a process, an evening dress
searching for what is and what is not.
Here's a thought: do you tell
the homeless man that his elaborate plan
to off himself is in itself a suicide, or did you decide
that death is necessary
for there to be a loss of life?

Depression isn't something you snap
out of. It's not another day that went to crap.
It's no "pull yourself up by the bootstraps."
It's living for the "happy" table scraps.
"How dare you need a babysitter."
"Don't be such a quitter."
"Why don't you just write a poem about it?"

Maybe instead of assuming a residential home
as just an observation dome,
think about the tools it gives for life on the outside.

Sweet Pea

My love for you was never an act of defiance.
It wasn't out of spite against the church or my father.
   It wasn't to prove myself to Hospital Jesus or the postman.

It was the unfurling of soft sweet pea tendrils.
It was the dropping of red jasper into a bird bath
   and watching the ripples make an O across the bowl.

It was the greening of the heart chakra.
It was the barking out pulses of energy
   from the chest and into the fingertips.

It was the opening of the Tennessee irises.
It was the message of a hope, a life worth
   living another lonely afternoon.

Purple Sadness

Jack London covers his purple sadness in wolf fur.
My brother covers his grey sadness in push-ups.

I don't cover it - I leave it raw.
Toss it onto the kitchen counter and tenderize it.
Cry on the telephone driving home.

Pop a couple Xanax from the cabinet
when I feel too much is coming on -
that mozzarella stomach bug
that shreds my fingers until all they can do is shake.

Lane Mochow

We Are On a Riot

We are medicated maniacs
that bite benzos for breakfast.
We are fast-fighting nonexistent fires,
and noose wires sing us to sleep.
We are on a riot.

We are bipolar and broken.
Jesus has spoken: we need
Valium and a shot of tequila.
We play prison 5 card pick up
and tell ourselves it'll be
all over soon enough.
We are on a riot.

We shoot up dope at 15,
live at the shelter at 45,
and survive off of pity soup kitchens
and what we beg on the streets.
We buy shoes at Dollar General
and smash Goodwill plates
when we're frustrated.
We are on a riot.

We are done being treated
like a disease on society,
people horror movies are made of.
Bipolar, depressed, schizophrenic,
we are all people, just like you.
We are on a riot.

Tired

The riptide of drowsiness slides unnoticed
up the ankles, along the spine, drooping along the edge of the eyelids.
Thirteen minutes tick by, and it has taken over.
I become a homeless slump, at least not dirtying up
another church pew, God forbid.

My medication has been doing this to me since the summer,
when it didn't matter that the early afternoon slipped through fingertips,
forgotten in the pillowcase. These days, my eyes hang
as I guzzle another cheap coffee, hoping caffeine
will keep the beast of sleep away.
At least until I get through all this work.

My First Marriage

Count us: five
best friends, of course,
(that's how these things go)
grappled him.

One had each arm,
the Officiant
the Witness
and me: the Bride.

"You may now hug
the bride!" she shouts.
I hold him, and for that
moment, he is mine.

Then, of course,
we release him, and
he runs
(that's how these things go).

Gasoline

The 5 gallon can of gasoline
Sloshes from my hand to yours.
Ideas stumble about the back of my head worse than any drunk.
Telling myself it must be for the truck
It must be for the lawnmower
It must be
It must be
It must
And yet,
You turn to me
Look me in the eye
And build an arc with oil that finds itself
Every last drop drips
Down the hallway
In the bedroom
In the kitchen
In the living room
Up the stairway to the attic
In the kitchen
Where you find the match,
That drifts to the floor all too fast.
Too fast to pull you out.
Too fast to think.
Too fast to breathe.

It couldn't be my fault.
It must be my fault.
It was in your eyes.
Your eyes

Lane Mochow

His eyes
Did you see the stalemate in his eyes?

Every arc takes us away from someplace,
To someplace.
All I can do is pray it's better than here.

The Hospital

We are the ones that nobody likes to talk about.
The ones people make blockbuster horror movies about.
The ones with wispy snake-tongues and sneering teeth.
The ones whose minds are broken.

They crop out the fact that we learn to cope
better than the people trusted with ballpoint pens.
Instead, they show our plastic zip-ties for "shoelaces",
Show we can't be trusted with safety scissors.
We do crosswords until our brains collapse;
maybe that'll keep us sharp.

Lane Mochow

Frantic

Frantic fingertips scratch circles on the back of your head. You shift from one foot to the other, thumping in your chest at all the things you need to get done, and all the things you haven't.

You can print mechanical representation of Chlorine Pentafluoride. I'll swing my legs off the back of your pickup truck, and contemplate the weight you're pulling behind you, a Radio Flyer full of listless tasks.

When I was in high school I tried to squeeze into two months every possible summer occupation: going to drive-in movies with you, swimming in a chlorine pool with you, parking your truck in a field at night to gape at the ethereal open sky, laughing with you until I couldn't breathe. We found time for the flickers of beauty, kept it in our cupped hands. We worked, but we were never panicked. Everything was what it was.

Today, you scrambled to class, to the therapist, back to class, to lunch, and to our de-stress hike. It wasn't until we were immersed, sweat licked up quickly by the chilly breeze, that you began to loosen the tension in your neck. Once we had taken you away, you were free again, chatting about dreams of the Appalachian Trail. Now, it's 11:30 in the evening, you've eaten macaroni and cheese and chugged a large coffee and are bonding chemical charts like a Japanese matchmaking computer game. You roll your neck because the tension's nestled itself back into its favorite spot. There are moments when you are lighthearted, and I feel like I've won, even for a little while.

We work, but there are still glimmers of those beautiful intimate moments. The ones that bring tears to my eyes in your arms on Tuesday evenings lying in bed. Everything still is what it is.

Lane Mochow

Pepper Spray

Two weeks after my 16th birthday I got my big present,
A russet car key pepper spray.
Why is it that
Just from that sentence you can tell I'm transgender?

My grandfather said it would give him peace of mind,
Because having a car means being alone
And being alone means raped.
And ya know what?
We are simply expected to deal with it.
That's our reality now.

But it isn't that we necessarily like it.
We call it "rape culture".
Hand rape an awareness month, tie it up in a red bow.
Give it a book,
A television show,
A punk song,
But don't dare call it normalized.
But the fact of the matter is ... it is.

We know the horror stories.
It's my mother at a party,
It's best friends and a guy we knew from middle school,
It's a partner who don't understand that a second date
doesn't equate to whatever you want whenever you want it.
It's a cycle,
It's "walk fast to your car in the unlit parking lot."

Well ya know what?
No.
I'm done.
I'm not hiding anymore.
I'm not afraid of death, nor life, nor angels, nor principalities.
I'm through.
Hang me in the courtyard by the jockstrap and call it justice.
I'm through.
Cut my shorts and call me easy.
I'm through.
I'm through wrapping myself in duct tape turtlenecks
    and calling it safe.
I'm through assuming men are beasts to fear, or that
    the beasts do not exist.
I'm through pretending everything is ok.
I'm through being told I'm being too "Feminist" or "Liberal"
Because I don't want to stay at home
Because I'm afraid to be seen alone, vulnerable.
I'm through being prey.
I'm through being afraid of becoming prey

Azaleas

If I sent you an armful of Azaleas
Fresh picked from the neighbor's backyard
You might think "How pretty."
That's about as far as it would go.
Little do you know Azaleas
Mean *fragile and ephemeral passion*,
The kind of love we used to have
When seventeen meant picking daisies-
Innocence- on the side of the highway.
That love is not lost, no,
But instead replaced by a more
Tennessee Dogwood-like tenderness,
Love undiminished by adversity,
Whose soft and white tipped petals
Embrace their thorns tips with grace.

A Garden

I want to plant an herb garden. Grow the seeds, watch their sweet germination. I want to be waiting patiently, hands in my lap, for the thyme and basil to wriggle up through the potting soil. I'd caress the single supple leaf of the sprout. I want to name them; fall in love with their sturdy stalks. I want to cheer them on when they reach up for the stars with their green fingers in the window. I'd water and listen to them from my brown paisley sheets, reading Vonnegut and sipping chamomile tea on a rainy Sunday afternoon, feeling the rich energy of life.

Saltamus

Kiss me and *saltamus* across the floor
in a Starbucks, put the baristas
in a freak-out - half awe and half begrudged.
Let them wonder what we do
when no one's around to watch.

Fold laundry with me, and spin-hang clothes
across the floor in the dorm, blasting Frank Sinatra
from the Bluetooth stereo, choose to never
think about in a few months, when we will
have to dance by ourselves over Skype.
"You'll make it work" they say, but I can't
even trust my own head or I'll pet cats
that don't actually exist
in the parking lot of Waffle House.

Put your head on my shoulder and pinky promise
you'll still love me when the voices
in my mind tell me the mafia wants my head,
and to drink vinegar and pack
three months' worth of food until
all I hear is silence on the telephone wires.

Kudzu

She was kudzu.
Originally, she was an other-worldly gift,
but she grew and grew, choking out
all the Black-Eyed Susans and Queen Anne's Lace.
She stretched her vines over every inch of my skin,
but claimed she didn't want to make it hers.
It was hers.

Once I realized I had let her take me over,
I took back my body with a chainsaw,
Slicing off of me the pads of her fingertips.
Watching her body fall to the floor, I left.
I don't regret taking my body back.
It's mine.

Lane Mochow

The Bonnaroo Tattoo

You and I propped ourselves against dusty trees,
and heard the thumping and bustling - the hubbub
of people all going somewhere, doing something.
Looking like a line of ants after you squish one,
they scramble to be anywhere and everywhere else.
You are unperturbed, now older and quieter
than the first time you were here, full of frantic energy.
Now you bob your head to a music far off,
humming the words you can't quite remember.

You'd never guess in a few months we'd be etching
that moment into the second layer of skin on our
   shoulder blades.
Memories sit so well beneath the skin,
hole up and sleep there, exposed and unabashed.

Things I Have Never Understood

I've never understood
global warming.
That just because
cows and terminates rip one,
that ratty diesel cars
and smokestacks
and cigarette butts in landfills
are m e l t i n g polar ice caps,
killing coral reefs, I am the true cause,
and therefore ought to feel guilty.

Maybe you and I are the reason,
(I'm sure any God-fearing man would agree)
because with you the
candles m e l t
and backs arch
at such a degree
that even my cat sweats
with the rise in temperature.

I've never understood how I could be
millions of miles away from the sun, and yet
when you kiss my neck, I swear
my knuckles
brush
against the planets.

I've never understood why I ended up
with a someone that brings out

Lane Mochow

every star in the universe
when his fingers
blaze
trails
along my skin,
but I wouldn't trade him for anything.

Stars

Stars can't write in Petroglyphs.
Can't tell folktales-
No ribs of cave walls smattered with char and grit.
Can't sneak out late after the world quiets to walk
  the streets with a summer love.
Can't yawn loneliness.
Can't marry.
Can't divorce.
Only giant-hood.
Only birth and death.
In an explosion NASA speculated
And no one remembered.

But when the stars are seen, when
Back is against a rough park bench
That can't quite kiss Death Valley
For a grimy gas station,
We begin to see them.
Truly see them.

And none can help but ramble on a naive attempt
  at deeper meaning.
So we point and try to puzzle-piece the Milky Way,
But gas is gas and space is space.
And for some the two spark awe.
And for some the two spark fear.
And for some the two spark research.
And for some the two spark the hot and heavy.
And for me, the two are the spark for them all.

Lane Mochow

For me
For you
Hell, for Hitler!

Because we are made of stars.
They stitch each of our fingertips
And the butterflies in our stomachs
When our fingers find another's.
They are our beginning,
Our end,
Our spark,
Our burn,
Our remembrance.

Ink

about the author

Lane Mochow is a young poet attending Tennessee Technological University with a major in Professional and Technical Communications with a minor in Art. When he is not writing, he enjoys painting, reading, and playing ukulele.

colophon

Ink, by Lane Mochow,
was set with Trebuchet MS fonts
by SpiNDec, Port Saint Lucie, Florida
The jacket and covers were designed by
Kris Haggblom, Port Saint Lucie, Florida

Publications from Poetic Justice Books

Growing Up Holy and Alone [3/2020]
by Adam Levon Brown

Broken Lines [1/2020]
by Isor Baridakara Deezua

Dear Miss B
by Dominic Albanese

The Phenomenal Human
by Ngozi Olivia Osuoha

Things Get Weird in Whistlestop
by Julie Carpenter

xenophobicracy
by Ngozi Olivia Osuoha

The Grey Revolution
by Ahmad Al-Khatat

If It Wasn't for the Earwigs, I'd Be Deaf
by Rose Aiello-Morales

Dead Man's Hand
by Jeff Weddle

Princes & Tides
by Dawn Taggblom

NDN: the words of a little hawk
by Elaine Gerard

Collecting Stars from a Night's Sky
by Clifford Benjamin Oppong

The Black Rose
by Kris Haggblom

The Last Beach Night
by Richard Pruitt

Riding Bareback Backwards
by Christina Quinn

The Death of Disco
by Alicia Young

Break
by Adam Levon Brown

Smile
by Alfred Gremsley

Ten Tiny Tales of Terrible War
by David Teinter

By Some Happenstance
by Dominic Albanese

Tales of Lord Su
by I Kyūu

For Those Who Don't Know Chocolate
by Amirah al Wassif

Hammer of God
by Aria Ligi

Visit https://www.poeticjusticebooks.com/PoeticJusticePress
for information and to order our latest titles

www.ingramcontent.com/pod-product-compliance
Lightning Source LLC
Chambersburg PA
CBHW030135100526
44591CB00009B/666